A

BRIEF

HISTORY

OF

MAURICE

TO THE THREE PEOPLE
WHO MAKE ME A BETTER
PERSON, I NEED NOT SAY
WHO YOU ARE, I DEDICTE
THIS BOOK TO YOU.

ALSO TO ALL THE PEOPLE WHO
HAVE ENTERED MY LIFE ALONG
THIS JOURNEY NEGATIVE OR
POSITIVE I OWE YOU A DEBT
THAT CANNOT BE REPAID.

SPECIAL THANKS TO MY FRIEND SAMY OUEDRAOGO
FOR THE IMAGES.

Preface

Have you ever thought about things, actually thought about things that you have done and haven't done in your life, just pause for a moment and think about all the positives and the negatives you've done on this journey we call life. About all the things you have achieved and places you have been and competitions you have won or for that fact lost? What about the people you have met along the way or rubbed shoulders with?

The ones you made smile and at the same time the ones you made cry? The ones we helped and the ones we chose not to, the ones we liked and the ones we didn't, how about the ones we loved and spent time with and the ones we lost along the way or let slip through our fingers like sand in an hour glass?

So many things, and people have passed through our lives but yet we choose to reminisce rather than to pay homage to those people, the places and the things that have shaped us into what we are today we just forget about. So many memories are in the distance, nearly forgotten about just fading into the back ground of our brains soon to become extinct. Well I'm not about to let that happen, the good the bad and the ugly no holding back, everyone of those important or unimportant shall be part of this book because whether they were a positive or a negative force in your life they have inadvertently shaped you to the person that you are today and many of them shall continue to shape you till the day we bid farewell to this rollercoaster ride labelled life.

And here the memoirs begin of a young gentleman, who from now on will be known as Maurice the monkey.

CHAPTER 1
THE DINGO

Dingo – *Canis lupus familiaris subspecies* that has **never been fully domesticated**. They adapted quite well to the harsh Australian wilderness, becoming the largest mammal predator there. As a wild animal, the *Dingo* is an **extremely efficient predator**, *who can hunt alone or in small groups.* **Dingo dog characteristics** are *high intelligence, resourcefulness, agility, independence, curiosity, alertness, boldness, stubbornness, sneaky, and disloyalty.*

__Weak and old members of the group will be deprived of food. Death due to starvation is efficient way for the pack to eliminate "useless" members of the group.__

How to begin? A long time ago? Way back when? Back in the good old days, A hop, skip and a jump back in time? Anyways let's crack on, we are going back to the year 1981 when it all began and the arrival of a baby monkey by the name of Maurice and his first appearance in the grand scheme of things. Born into a working class western Irish family in a small coastal town by the name of Sligo was where Maurice would take his first baby steps and where he would draw on the people around him for guidance and show him the way as he endeavoured along his path to manhood.

His Daddy, a short, stocky, rather plump moustached, chain smoking gentleman was a blue collar worker with a wicked temper and a loose fist.

His Mommy a short plump lady with a heart of gold and your typical Irish mammy both who work hard every day to put clothes on his back and food on the table.

His relationship with his father wasn't exactly the normal type being in an all male household there wasn't much room for shows of affection or hugs if you know what I mean, as for his relationship with his mother this was slightly better as she occasional showed him some love but like I said this was the 80's and things were tough people had to work hard and had less time for the softer more gentle things in life especially with young boys.

As I stated previously things in Ireland in the 80's were tough due to the lack of jobs and low earnings, parents worked from hand to mouth and this is how life was, it wasn't until years later would the effect of the "Celtic Tiger" would become visible so let's take a look back in time and explain the younger years of this little monkey. Maurice grew up in the presence of his two brothers, one older and one younger. As a young monkey he looked up to his big brother as a role model but soon found that his big brother had other things on his mind other than looking after his little bro, his elder brother had females on his mind and usually hung out with his older friends and didn't have much time for Maurice, alternatively he then looked to his younger brother and soon found out that it wasn't cool for the younger brother to hang out with his older brother.

You could say this was to define his younger years, he was always kind of stuck in the middle which was exactly his position in the family, this was to become the norm for young Maurice. He didn't much like being stuck in the middle and it was from the start an up-hill battle for him always striving to be noticed.

He quickly found out that he would have to search elsewhere. Maurice found himself looking to sport in order to find solace amongst others, to make friends and get the acceptance he craved so badly. Although Maurice excelled at sports and he took part in many a sporting activity he still hungered for something more, more than sports had to offer, there was a hunger inside him, a craving that he so desperately needed to fill but even he couldn't explain what it was. Even as he excelled at sports and won many accolades his family just seemed to ignore all of his achievements and put the mediocre achievements of his siblings above everything he had done which to say the least didn't go down well with Maurice. Not receiving the attention he desired only sped up his downward spiral.

Due to his monkey character he continuously found himself dabbling and rubbing shoulders with the wrong people which only distanced himself further from his kin but this is the attention he yearned for that he desired so much it's what he searched for. For him it was like his own secret rebellion, and the same time deep inside he was never fulfilled and deep inside a constant craving burned, he had found what he had been looking for but yet the yearning grew and grew. He was hoping to fill in the years of being left out and he wouldn't stop until he had it.

He continued excelling at sports making all types of teams and picking up winners medals for numerous competitions but this still wasn't enough to satisfy that insatiable itch he had inside for attention, he needed more...

During this difficult period he had a shameful and embarrassing secret that only his family knew about, up until his teenage years Maurice was a chronic bed wetter and he never knew why, it was very difficult for him to come to terms with and he hid a quiet anger with himself and a deep disliking to himself also, he visited many a doctor but yet the reason was never diagnosed as to why it was happening and why he couldn't stop, there were many theories as to why this was happening but still no concrete answer came to light, due to this disorder Maurice had some small issues with body odour which made it even harder for him to fit in. Many of the kids in school noticed this and he received many an insult as he grew up, not only because of his body odour but also due to the fact Maurice had bright red fur which led to his nickname as a child:

RED HOWLER MONKEY....

So, soon he noticed that he found it difficult to make friends and more commonly he made enemies and got into many a scuffle, on a daily basis Maurice got into at least one fight. Due to his red coloured fur things were even harder for this young feral monkey and damn did he have a temper on and off the pitch. He fought on the pitch, in school and on the street with anybody who challenged him or offended him and boy he was easily offended, one might say he lost his temper exceedingly quick. He was forever getting into trouble and sometimes even breaking the law but you know what they say about middle kids, they sometimes push things to the limit to get some attention from the people around them and Maurice knew no better.

As he progressed into his teenage years the problems continued and the level of misdemeanours grew, from problems within the family to problems in the neighbourhood and even problems with the police. Ok now he wasn't only getting into trouble, he did have his quiet times and also his successful times in his life and of course there were a handful of friends he could always rely on but not just friends he had girlfriends too which helped as a distraction but just like his lightening quick temper those girls changed as quickly as the weather and in hindsight looking back at these such young girls they were probably better off because at this age

Maurice still had a lot of learning and growing up to do mentally and physically ☺

Like I previously mentioned he was rubbing shoulders with the wrong people and this is where he got himself into very hot water indeed. As a youngster he had stolen small things and broken the occasional window or even steal a bike or two but nothing would compare to what was about to happen next and it would shape his relationship with his family forever to this day it still lingers like a metaphorical fly around shite....💩💩💩

Of course being a young monkey and full of confidence he thought that he could get away with anything and the more he got away with the more his confidence grew and at one point he even felt invincible and that he would never get caught. This is one lesson you should always be aware of:

THE MORE YOU GET AWAY WITH THE MORE YOU ARE BEING WATCHED SO ALWAY BEHAVE LIKE YOU ARE JUST ABOUT TO BE CAUGHT....

And here is the first encounter that would change the path of Maurice's life and in terms of his relationship with his family for the worse, one might say an irreparable but I wouldn't say unforgivable mishap. ☹

Maurice re-established a childhood friendship, with a guy who he hadn't seen or heard from for a very long time due to the fact he had lived down under for many moons. Owing to this small piece of Information he shall be known as 'THE DINGO'. This friendship was to change the course of Maurice's path to manhood massively and in quite a negative fashion but as they say "we don't learn from the things we do correctly"

The Dingo came cruising back into the village with an air of slickness and suave, he had his hair dyed dark black, he had a cobra tattooed on his lower arm and wore quite outlandish bright clothing, something the village folk couldn't comprehend or in fact had never seen before but at the same time were in awe of the hairstyle the muscles and the quirky fashion and Maurice was taken in without even realising. The Dingo had a presence about him and he could see he was the cool Cat in the village and when the chance came along for Maurice to hang out with the Dingo the naive little monkey grabbed his chance with both hands, this is what Maurice had been craving most of his childhood, to be part of the gang that everybody wanted to be part of and he wasn't about to miss out.

They hung out, they partied, they picked up chicks and all the other things that was cool to do, but unbeknownst to the little monkey the Dingo was strategically setting Maurice up to take the fall and the whole friendship was a facade and just a stepping stone in the plan the Dingo was hatching.

Maurice had spent his entire life up to this point in this quiet little seaside village and knew the daily on goings of its inhabitants pretty well but he never thought he would be manipulated into harming any of them and he also believed that nobody would want such useless information.

The Dingo slyly and subconsciously extracted knowledge about all the ongoing activities in the small village and started to collect information for a group of unknown men to Maurice but as far as Maurice thought he was just being cool and doing what he thought would help him fit in.

The Dingo asked and asked for more details and more details, minutes, hours, times, days and every piece of information he could get all out of the foolish little monkey. Then the Dingo focused his questions on one enterprise within the village 'the caravan park' and of course Maurice having spent a lot of his childhood hanging around this area knew the answers to most of the questions and gave them willingly, unsuspecting of what was about to happen next....

A couple of days had passed without anything to write home about when one evening the little monkey received a curious and cryptic SMS from the Dingo. The SMS read: *'Maurice' gotta keep my head down, trying to stay under the radar, don't write back to this number check the local papers wait for contact. Dingo.* Now imagine yourself in this situation and your so called close friend writes a message like he's a member of some secret organisation, clearly you would think that your friend is off his rocker and has been smoking far too much weed and the paranoia has finally got the better of him?

He was soon to find out that what the Dingo had been telling him was far from paranoia and was actually a real situation and his actions with the SMS and the strange behaviour were justified....

Maurice was perplexed, it was all so very confusing for him what the Dingo was talking about but he duly picked up all the local papers and began scanning for something that would explain the Dingo's odd behaviour. And there it was the reason for all the questions and the reason for all the chats before the reason for the friendship. A small story hidden on the inside of the paper. For some it was a small insignificant story but for Maurice it might as well have been on the front page in capital, bold letters **<u>CARAVAN PARK HEIST</u>**😲😲😲..

Maurice couldn't believe what he was reading as he read the story over and over again, the details of what had happened were as if he had been there himself instructing the whole incident like a conductor in an orchestra (He wasn't!!). He tried to contact the Dingo on numerous occasions but nothing, he went to his house and nothing it was like he never existed and Maurice was worried. Think about it – you are like seventeen years old and some cool guy returns to the village and befriends you and little do you know that you are just a stepping stone in his master plan, how do you think a seventeen year old who has only been in trouble with his parents in the past and with neighbours for breaking windows is going to feel knowing that he would now potentially be facing criminal charges for his unknowing involvement in something far more serious????

It wasn't until three to four days after the story had been printed in the papers that the Dingo finally touched base. This time from an unknown number and again a very cryptic massage. *'Railway bar 12.00, don't be late don't tell anyone where you are going!!!'*

Maurice wasn't sure what to think but he knew he had to find out what had gone down and what really was his involvement because what had taken place a few nights earlier had very serious consequences.

He arrived on time in the chosen location and scanned the bar for the Dingo. Out of the corner of his eye he seen a large hand waving at him from one of the small enclaves at the back of the bar, upon closer inspection he seen it was the Dingo! He approached slowly taking in his surrounding to see who was accompanying him and he seen a peculiar old grandfather like man sitting next to him wearing glasses, drinking tea and reading the paper. The Dingo ushered Maurice to sit. Maurice had so many questions but the old man stopped him in his tracks and hushed him. The first words out of his mouth were *'did you speak to anybody?'* followed by *'have the police been in contact?'* then followed by the chilling sentence *'we know where you live Maurice and if we get caught you are coming down with us'.*

Shock!! Maurice felt physically sick, scared and shaking he agreed with the old man and swore not to say anything. As he left the bar he couldn't help but think he technically hadn't done anything wrong that he actually didn't know that such a crime was about to be perpetrated and that he wasn't there when it happened but Maurice was about to learn one of his most valuable life lessons.

He travelled home with the Dingo in the car and the Dingo told him exactly what had happened a few nights previously. He went into detail of the whole ordeal and about how he was driving the car for the scoundrels who carried out the deed, about how he and his little gang scoped out the caravan park for days hence no contact from the Dingo, also how they had followed the owner of the caravan park home one evening so they knew exactly where he lived and how on the night it all happened, how they broke into his house and waited for him to come home, tie him up, steal his van and keys and proceeded to the caravan park to open the safe and of course how they took the cash registers.

Maurice was flabbergasted, gobsmacked to say the least. Once the Dingo had finished detailing what had happened. The Dingo dropped him off at his home and Maurice for the rest of the day couldn't even look at food he was as they say 'sick with worry' and would you blame the poor little monkey? What had he gotten himself into this time???

A few days passed worryingly and quite uncomfortably for the little monkey. During this time Maurice had continued to squander time with the Dingo. And then it happened, one nice Irish summer afternoon Maurice had returned home from work and was tidying his room when there was a knock on the door. He went down stairs only to see two sullen looking gentlemen at his door. They quickly showed their police badges and asked if they were speaking to Maurice the monkey which he responded they were. That asked some questions about the Dingo and his colleagues, also about the caravan park and it's owner and about the incident which had taken place a fortnight ago.

Maurice knew his rights and refused to answer any of the questions especially since the officers had just randomly shown up on his doorstep and he wasn't being arrested because he in fact had no physical connection to the fiasco itself. The police however pointed out that there was proof that Maurice had been travelling in a vehicle which was used as a get-away car in a crime and that it contained stolen items which made him an accomplice to a crime and to make things worse the police informed him that the Dingo had already visited them and told them his side of the story at this point the little monkey knew that the Dingo was selling him down the river for immunity.☹

All Maurice could think about was about how his new best friend who he had taken to so quickly, who he trusted so much had stabbed him in the back and went to the police and implicated him in a crime that he had literally very little to do with. According to the police the Dingo told them that it was because of the information Maurice had given made the heist possible but Maurice didn't even know his answers were being used for such an unspeakable crime, if he had known he would never had given such information and would have tried to talk the Dingo out of ever committing it.

But now it was too late for that, the Dingo had played his cards very close to his chest but was now revealing them to the police and was using Maurice as his "get out of jail free card"

Maurice returned to his bedroom and began to think and question what his next move would be. He came to the conclusion that if the police did indeed have proof that he had been an accomplice that it would in his favour if he was the one to tell the police and not for the police to tell him, and that's exactly what he done. He jumped on his scooter and didn't stop for anything until he reached the police station where he sat down and told the police how naive he had been and how he had been taken advantage of by sharper, cuter, smooth talking characters.

The police in fact felt sorry for Maurice and told him how fucking stupid he had been but due to his involvement there would be a consequence to be paid. During this visit to the police Maurice learnt that the Dingo in order not to be punished gave all the names of the people involved and that the little monkeys name had intermittently been used but it confirmed to the police that the monkey didn't take part in the crime but had inadvertently given sensitive information without his knowledge but all the same it was still breaking the law.

Ok so now he had broken the law but he hasn't been directly involved more indirectly we can say but due to this he had to suffer the consequences. Of course this was his first misdemeanour which meant he wouldn't be receiving a criminal record of any sorts let's say more of a slap on the wrist for being such a fool, but the worst punishment he could receive was that which came from the same paper which informed him about the crime taking place itself because they had a practice to publish such court hearings as a form of social embarrassment, as a punishment to deter such foolish mistakes and of course Maurice's name and address and what had happened were published for all to see which in hand tarnished the family name forever, hence the beginning of the end for any hope Maurice had to get the attention or respect he had so badly craved as a little monkey from his family, he did in fact get attention but not the type he sought.....

The paper printed the story and soon everybody knew what had taken place and the extent of the involvement of the little monkey, and due to the fact the village was a small community it wasn't long before everyone knew and the whispers and the looks were hard to bare. Maurice knew he had to get away because he was no longer welcome and his family had given up on him because this time he had gone too far. His parents were utterly embarrassed and the rest of the family too including all of his local relatives from his aunts and uncles and cousins too. They didn't want to be associated with him and the made it very clear to the young monkey. He was in a sense shunned by the entire family.

His decision to leave was a form of self-banishment for the shame and embarrassment he had brought upon his unsuspecting family and friends something he had difficulty accepting so he packed up his things and hit the road. As for the Dingo, Maurice had no contact with him ever again and hasn't seen or spoken to him ever since.

See this was never what Maurice ever wanted even though he was always seen as a little monkey with a bad attitude and a short temper and all he ever wanted was to fit in and be accepted which was from the beginning as far as Maurice can remember an up-hill battle.

He never wanted to hurt anybody let alone be involved with the things he got caught up in but it happened and this is history it's just a shame not everybody sees it that way and Maurice has learnt that some people will never let go of grudge

The moral of this chapter is:

Trust your instincts and be aware of the actions and words you use because they may well just come back to haunt you. (Maurice learnt the hard way and is still paying for it.) Always know that some people will never let go of the things we have done to hurt them so there is not point especially with some people on bridging the gaps and you are better off just getting on with your life and believe me when I say this that such people you don't really need in your life anyways.

But if you are thinking that his family are being a bit harsh for holding a grudge for so long then you might have a point but if you think this is the only thing Maurice has done then you are mistaken.

There's more to come................ unfortunately.

CHAPTER 2
GREENER FIELDS

Ok so he had alienated himself from his friends and family and lost all respect even though there wasn't much to begin with, he had lost it and there was no going back, he had done what he had done and as much as he would have wanted too there is just no turning back time. It was time for Maurice to start looking out for himself cause no one else was going to do it for him.

He thought to himself that given time his family would forgive and forget but he was and still is a metaphorical 'splinter in their behinds' and as much as they wish it would go away Maurice was still their blood which couldn't be ignored. Maurice hit the road and took up jobs in different places and cities until he finally settled in a larger town where no one knew him and he had some type of anonymity where he could start again and rebuild himself they way he wanted to and nobody would know any different. So he started again, he worked hard and he studied and he kept this going until in his work he was beginning to make a name for himself. He had found a job he was perfect fit for him.

Maurice always had a way with words and as they say in Ireland he had 'The gift of the gab' if you are reading and you don't know what that is it's basically, if speaking was an Olympic sport this kid would without doubt make the winner's podium every time. Maurice always knew what to say, when to say and how to say it. He had a way with words that his family mistrusted in him but for people who didn't know him trusted him instantly. He used this gift in work to charm his colleagues and his bosses over the years but he found out that this gift of being able to manipulate words worked best on the female sex and he used it to the best of his abilities.

He played football and he worked hard and he studied hard and he began to become someone, and occasionally he went home but it was always pretty uncomfortable for him and his family and he felt it, trust me nobody was really trying to hide it and why should they, especially after what he had done to them and to the family name I guess in some sense it was just desserts.

In work he was promoted time after time until he was assistant manager in the office and soon he was training staff teaching them his way, his style, his tricks and he built up a very strong team one that was smashing company records all over the country in regards to sales. He picked up awards and travelled all over Europe teaching and talking and giving advice on how he made sales something easy. His boss was so impressed he put him up for promotion again this time it was a position in the Netherlands as company trainer. He took the job but he never really enjoyed his time and he soon returned to the his little island. When he came back after a few months away he took a job and quite surprisingly it was for a charitable organisation and what better way to give back a little after having took so much.

So as always no matter what Maurice had done in his life he always wanted to be the best at it and better than everybody else, I guess we can say he had a bit of a competitive streak in him. This job however was pretty peculiar, it involved standing on the street with a little table and a handful of scratch cards that were sold by convincing passers-by to donate to charity and have the chance to win something. You might think that this is easy but it's not especially when people questioned your reasons for doing so whether you were driven by profit or by wanting to help the misfortunate. In Maurice's case it was a bit of both plus this job gave him the opportunity to remain anonymous and the chance to travel around Ireland and experience his own country first hand which was at the time the perfect fit. It was through this job that Maurice would encounter the next person who would change his life forever.....

But we will get to that person in chapter three, Maurice continued his work, made lots of friends and rarely visited his little village on the coast. He saved his money and he continued to work hard. Not long after his boss approached him and asked him to take on a similar role which he had previously held in his former company. So Maurice became a trainer again and it was his job to teach newbies the tricks of the trade which he had a great knack for. So he trained and he trained people until one day his boss said he had a test for him. Maurice was receive two foreign trainees and it was his job to prepare them for the Irish streets and speaking to

Irish people. His response? He didn't even bat an eye ☺

So the training began and this is where Maurice met the next person that would influence the direction his life would take for the rest of his life not that Maurice looked at it like that but that's what was about to happen. Not long after taking the job working for a charity Maurice seen an ad in the local paper for bearded men to work as an extra in an upcoming Hollywood movie which was due to commence filming in Ireland. Maurice applied and within a few days found himself on the set of a movie.

But that's a story for another day....

CHAPTER 3

THE PRAYING MANTIS

Mantid (family Mantidae) – the first thing that we can relate to
a **praying mantis** is controlling. Also, this insect may be a symbol
of mindfulness and control. The symbolism of this insect also
includes patience, awareness, intuition and creativity, going crazy
sometimes, aggression towards males. They have triangular heads
with bulging eyes supported on flexible necks. Females sometimes
practice **sexual cannibalism**, eating their mates after copulation.

So that week Maurice took on two new apprentices to train into the job. To his surprise they turned out to be two young recently graduated eastern European girls. He thought to himself that they were weird and strange and that that they would never be able to part Irish folk from their hard earned Euros. He had a few reasons as to why he thought they would ever succeed at doing so.

One because they had strange accents when they spoke English and Maurice felt that Irish people wouldn't understand them and secondly Irish people are quite sceptical to charities in general and even more so if the person collecting is not Irish themselves... But nevertheless Maurice had a job to do and by God he was going to give it a go.

He versed them, he repeated again and again and he tested them until they were street ready. Then the day came to send them out alone on the streets of Ireland. He kept a close eye on his fledglings and he kept in contact with them throughout the day to encourage them to keep going. At sunset he rang the young padawans and told them to finish up for the day and return to base. When they arrived back they both had exceeded expectations and had collected quite a sum of money, in fact more than any other volunteer on their first day. When Maurice told his supervisor he told them that they deserved some special recognition and he paid for their drinks and their dinner that evening to the excitement of the two trainees.

That evening Maurice with the tidy sum of fiscal help from his boss wined and dined the girls (Guinness and burgers ;)) At this stage Maurice had grown pretty fond of the two trainees and he was wondering if or not he should voice his opinion especially about the blonde one. So he decided that as the girls were consuming alcohol by the bucket load he would use it as a way to extract information that would help him in seducing this young lady. He began flirting and giving compliments throughout the evening and then at one point the brunette said to Maurice whilst the blonde was in the bathroom that what he was doing was cute but they both knew what he was attempting and that there was no need cause the blonde was interested in him too. 😄

And so the next part of the relationship began between the little monkey and the Mantis. They began dating, growing closer every day and learning about one another. This is Maurice actually needed in his life at this time. A smart, well educated partner that would help him and appreciate what he had to offer but little did he know that this only stretched as far as the boarder of his homeland and later he would find out what was in store for him. He didn't take into consideration that the Mantis was on holidays and that her behaviour wasn't the full extent of her character (but don't forget the title of the first book: the silly monkey!!) All things considered Maurice was having a great time and falling in love for the first time in his life. The relationship grew and grew and they were having the time of their lives. Not long after they were offered a new job on the set of a movie which they thought would be fun and so they both agreed to go for it.

In order for the Mantis to get a job they had to pretend that they were a newlywed couple and that they had just arrived in Ireland without their marriage certificate which the production company fell for and the Mantis became Mantis the monkey and Maurice used his social security number so she could pay taxes legally. They spent three months on the set of the movie and living in a tent (not the most hygienic, trust me), due to the fact they were living in a tent it allowed them to save everything they were earning for the work they were carrying out. When productions finished they both had saved a considerable sum of money but at the same time their Indian summer was coming to an end and the Mantis was coming to the end of her sabbatical abroad.

Decisions decisions, they were left with a choice but what he didn't know at this particular time was that the decision he was about to make would alter the direction and path of his life incomprehensibly.

So they sat down and they discussed the possibilities.

1. *Break up.*
2. *Long distance relation.*
3. *Move to Eastern Europe.*

In the end Maurice choose the latter and one day after his twenty second birthday Maurice packed his suitcase and jumped on a bus to Dublin where he would Catch a flight to London, wait a few hours and Catch another plane to one of Europe's most beautiful medieval cities in Eastern Europe, Prague, Czech Republic was the destination.

This was where he would reunite with his love the Mantis. They spent three magnificent days in this wonderful city full of ancient castles and a famous bridge which was used in a James bond movie. They spent the days like royalty, Maurice trying all the delicacies of this eastern land. After their stay they jumped on a bus and began travelling to the homeland of the Mantis. This would be how Maurice got introduced to a country which would become his second home or his adoptive country. They arrived under the cover of night where a tall dark strong looking man was waiting for them as they got off the bus. It was the father of the Mantis. He offered his enormous hand to the little monkey as a form of greeting and muttered something in the local language. Maurice took it as a greeting but it just as well could have been an insult 😄. They stowed the bags away into the car and drove to their home on the other side of the city.

The next morning Maurice was introduced to the rest of the family and also the local breakfast which to him was completely new to him. The locals practiced eating slices of bread with cucumber, tomatoes and cheese and a sprinkle of salt accompanied by a cup of fruit flavoured tea all of which to Maurice was completely bizarre but there was more bizarre to come. One thing he couldn't get his head around was why the locals insisted on taking off their shoes when entering the house and replacing them with slippers. They tried to explain that it was in order to keep the floors clean and stop their feet becoming too hot when in fact to Maurice wiping your shoes upon entrance would suffice and putting on warm slippers didn't make your feet any cooler at home but he didn't argue. In relation to the bizarre situations one arose in regards to this exact tradition of putting on slippers.

One evening Maurice returned back to the house and the father who of course was trying to be kind and polite offered his warm sweaty slippers to the little monkey, he politely declined and if you had seen the condition of the fathers feet you would have declined too 😄

Maurice was pretty new to this country and wasn't quite sure what type of work he would do whilst he was there but in the end correlating to the fact he didn't speak the local language he ended up lecturing in his own language. Initially he was pretty scared of such a task but if you remember from previous chapters in this book it didn't take him very long to get the hang of it and he was soon a very popular teacher of the English language.

Maurice had no idea what length of time he would spend in this strange, exotic land but he did know that he felt quite comfortable here because of the adoration of his loving students and also the attention he received from the locals because he was a native English speaker.

Whenever he went out with friends it was never difficult to start up a conversation with the locals. One question he kept getting was: *Why Poland??* He always responded by saying there were too many Poles in Ireland so he jumped on plane to get away but got on the wrong fucking plane :-p

Maurice really enjoyed the attention he was receiving. He enjoyed being the life and soul of the party and the conversation he was living it up, soaking it all up while it lasted and why not?

Many years passed and Maurice had settled in quite well to his surrounding and he was even picking up the language pretty quickly and in general things were going quite swimmingly.

However they say every dark cloud has a silver lining well if that's the case then ever silver lining has a dark cloud and the clouds were beginning to gather. He noticed as every day passed the Mantis was becoming more and more distant and less affectionate towards him and that she was more focussed on her career rather than her relationship. I mean to be honest their courtship had always been tempestuous and had it's up and downs but now it was coming to an abrupt halt and would never be the same again.

In all relationships there will be ups and downs and of course people who love each other will say and do things to hurt each other, we kind of get caught up in all the anger and we forget to realise that the person we are harming will in the long run be the person we love and care for and it will all come full circle and we too will eventually be hurt by our own actions and words. I guess it's kind of cliché but in fact it's also the truth:

"TREAT OTHERS HOW WE WANT TO BE TREATED"

One of the biggest reasons for this was the decision Maurice and the Mantis had made to have offspring and after the children had been born the Mantis put more time into her work than ever before leaving poor little old Maurice looking after two toddlers in the morning and working as a lecturer in the evenings and when he had the opportunity to get some downtime the Mantis wanted to go somewhere or do something which didn't really work.

This is not one of Maurice's proudest moments but he was young and naive and we all make mistakes. Instead of trying to alleviate the situation he began to rebel against the demands of the Mantis. He would go out drinking with his buddies after work and return home late in the hope that the Mantis would be sleeping and not waiting up for him. This just made matters worse and the arguments continued. They fought endlessly and at times it even became semi-violent not only on his behalf but the mantis too was no angel.

This went on for some time and the problems between the two escalated to the point that it was unbearable for them both and soon the decision was made that the Mantis and the little monkey would go their separate ways. Now you may be thinking how could Maurice just walk away from his kids well I guess that's because you don't really know him and in order to do so you must keep reading....

Maurice began to look for a new place and it wasn't long before he packed his bags and moved out of his first polish home. Now a lot of people once given such freedom would just go look for a fresh start in a new place but Maurice had done that once before but this time he had more responsibilities and he refused to let his little monkeys grow up without him in their lives. He would not be that type of monkey who had children and them just shirked his duties.

Maurice had made his mind up very quickly. He would remain in this strange land in order to see his kids grow up, to get to know them, for them to know their father, to play football with them, to have happy and memorable moments with them and to try and be involved as much as possible. After all these kids were his flesh and blood and he loved them dearly and one failed relationship wouldn't stop him from being there for them and making his little monkeys feel his love for them.

CHAPTER 4
THE BALD HEADED EAGLE

Eagles – tend to take care of younger or weaker Eagles which need help and will always protect them from predators. They make fantastic friends and partners. Eagles have large, hooked beaks and also Eagles have excellent eyesight for predicting and seeing trouble on its way.

Bald eagles aren't actually bald (sorry buddy).

So you may have noticed that so far in this brief history of Maurice it's been all difficult with a lot of turmoil and disappointments, bad decisions and negativity. Well there is a few people who have come into Maurice's life that made it better for once. This unit will focus on the guy Maurice likes to call his brother from a Polish mother.

As Maurice worked he made many an encounter with the local folk. One evening upon entering one of his classrooms prepared to teach and introduce himself to the group he immediately noticed that one of the students happened to be donning the jersey of his boyhood club 'Glasgow Celtic'. This he thought to himself was a man with good taste especially with football.

As things turned out the young gentleman who shall be known as the Eagle from now on was a really cool guy who loved Celtic and loved football just like Maurice. It wasn't long before their bond became stronger and soon they were going for pints, hanging out, going to parties and were hunting together (in night clubs for women).

The Eagle helped Maurice settle in Poland and if it wasn't for his friendship things would have been much more challenging for the little monkey.

He was also there for Maurice during the very difficult times he had with the Mantis, he also if Maurice Ever needed lent him cash during difficult financial times and whenever Maurice was too drunk to make it home the Eagle always gave him a couch to sleep on. Maurice knew he had made a friend for life and the Eagle was always there for him no matter what the problem.

The Eagle was always available to him and whenever Maurice had to change flats it was the Eagle who never said he was too busy to help. As you read the book and you read about the other encounters Maurice faced to get to where he is today the Eagle was never too far away and was always involved especially when Maurice needed him.

This is a short unit to pay homage to a friend who has always been there for Maurice and as they say sometimes less is best.

The moral of this short unit is as follows:

At the end of the day every man needs a good mate who he can rely on no matter what the situation and the Eagle is this mate for Maurice, he knows he can trust him with anything and that he will always be there for him. Maurice learnt that there are some people out there who genuinely care for him and will help him. So to anybody reading no matter how bad things may seem there is always somebody or some people who think about you and care about your wellbeing and all you have to do is let them know and they will be there for you...

(THANK YOU MICHAŁ FOR BEING MY FRIEND)

CHAPTER 5

+2 LITTLE MONKEYS

Monkey (primates) – fun, playful, curious, intelligent and always getting into trouble. These monkeys are famous for their "dawn chorus". These roaring and howling calls are performed mostly by the males in the group. **Red howlers** are the biggest of the **howler monkeys**. This **monkey** has thick, brownish to dark **red** fur, with gold or bright orange under parts, the colour varying with the age and where the animal lives. The naked dark face is surrounded by fur. They have a somewhat stubby nose and their wide jaw is covered in a thick beard.

This chapter will go into detail the ups and downs and the constant turmoil and difficulties Maurice has to deal with in order to be the father he wanted to be for his two little monkeys.

From court cases, to threats, to visits to the police station, to nearly being made homeless and to being absolutely penniless and having to count small change from a box where he kept all small coins just in case something like this ever happened in order to be able to afford to buy some bread. He had a very rough time but in his head these two little monkeys were the most important thing in his life and if this is how it was going to be then so be it and he was determined not to quit or give up on them. These two little monkeys are the next people in the brief history of Maurice and how once again life would change beyond recognition ☺.

No words can express the hurt and sadness Maurice had to deal with when he was waking up every day and not seeing his little monkeys, not hearing them call him and not playing with them. It's a very weird thing when a man has a baby people say the connection between mother and child is incomparable which I don't argue with but what most don't know is the connection between father and child is also a very special thing and Maurice felt this with his little monkeys. It hurt him deep to his core it was as if somebody had taken away toes on his feet causing him to be off balance all the time, this lack of balance was the disruption that was caused by not having his little monkeys around him every day.

It was an eternal struggle but something he knew he had to persist with in order to see his kids regularly. In the early days of the breakup things were pretty bad and Maurice had the feeling that the whole world was closing in around him and nobody was on his side. Thankfully Maurice had dealt with similar situations in his youth and he knew how to deal with this.

He would remain positive and keep fighting this was in his nature. At first the Mantis wouldn't answer phone calls or reply to messages and completely shut him out from any contact with the young ones but he kept trying and then after sometime she needed his help and she began to drop the kids off with him and pick them up in the evenings, other times she would bring them to her parents and Maurice if he wanted to spend time with them had to go there but it didn't faze him at all.

Things were about to get strange however, one lovely Saturday afternoon Maurice went over to the parents of the Mantis where the kids were. He had lunch with them and chatted about the plans for the day and then he politely told her father that he would be taking the kids back to his flat when he was rudely told 'NO' under no circumstances according the her father would Maurice be leaving with the little ones and the only way he would be leaving would be alone.

Maurice continued to be polite and once again told her father that this was his plan and that the kids would be leaving with him. Again he was told NO and this time the father of the Mantis tried to pull the younger monkey from Maurice's hands and made the baby cry!!

After this Maurice began to explain that they were his children and if he wanted to leave with them that the old man couldn't stop him. The old man began to shout and scream and insult and threaten Maurice and he said he would call the police if he tried to leave to which Maurice told him to do so because even though it wasn't his country he knew his rights. So Maurice packed up the kids belongings and left. He was shocked at the behaviour the old man had demonstrated in front of the young ones and he tried to calm the crying children down.

When he arrived back at the street where his flat was parked directly across the street was the father of the Mantis waiting for him!!! For Maurice it was bonkers and he couldn't understand this bizarre behaviour but it was something that would happen on a regular basis and Maurice soon learnt that it was he who was the problem due to the fact he was the foreigner and the locals were showing him who was boss. Worried and stressed Maurice locked his doors and kept watch over his offspring and played and fed them to make sure they were ok.

This continued for many years but Maurice was always one step ahead of the Mantis and her family. He knew he had to continue being polite and that things would eventually settle down. He would have many difficult situations and unfriendly encounters but this is what he had to deal with in order to be the father he wanted to be for his children. He had to deal with police many occasions about unfounded accusations and with debt collectors blocking his account and taking money from him and sending embarrassing letters to his place of work but he refused to lie down in fact this behaviour of the Mantis was only making the little monkey stronger and more resilient to her tactics.

Maurice suffered many a sleepless night and had many difficult days, weeks and months even difficult years. But he had made his decision to stand his ground not knowing he was building the foundations to his most important relationship between him and his two little monkeys, it would be one of the greatest decisions he had ever made.

The Mantis completely ignorant to her importance in the matter had inadvertently turned Maurice from a young, immature and foolish monkey into a strong, mature, caring, loving father and not only that she had really opened his eyes in relation to dealing with people and most importantly she had given him two amazing little monkeys with an unbreakable bond to this day.

So one has to be aware of the fact that even negative people in your life can provide you with a lifetime of happiness so with all the hatred and anger Maurice had towards the Mantis there is a massive debt of gratitude towards her too. Young Maurice had picked up many valuable life lessons from these experiences with the Mantis and at the same time added probably the two most important people into his life story.

To this day Maurice has a great bond with his little ones who are not so little any more but more will be told about these two little monkeys in later chapters ☺.

CHAPTER 6
THE WANNABE WISE OWL

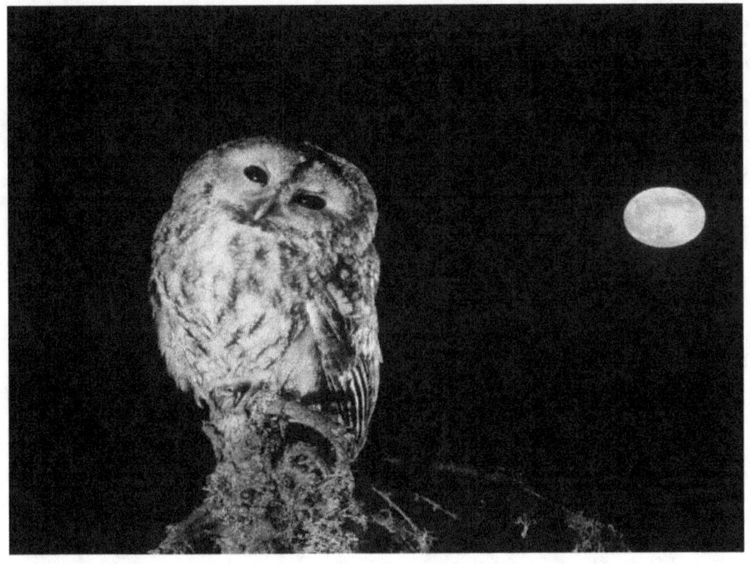

Owls (Strigiformes) – mostly solitary and nocturnal birds of prey typified by an upright stance, a large, broad head, binocular vision, binaural hearing, sharp talons, and feathers adapted for silent flight. Owls came to represent wisdom because of their large eyes.

Owls can turn their heads almost all the way around – but not quite. Because they can't do everything perfectly no matter how hard they try or believe they can....

So life went on Maurice had a strong relationship with his offspring and things slowly improved. The mantis and her family eased off and Maurice could finally get on with his life and have his kids close by too. He realised that every cloud does in fact have a silver lining and he believes to this day that this whole situation had given him strength to deal with anything life could possibly throw at him.

So now things were different, he had spent the last eight years of his life with the Mantis and finally he had broken free from that, there was the metaphorical weight off his shoulders. He was in a country full of beautiful women and to his surprise being an Irish monkey in eastern Europe was a kind of exotic thing for the local ladies and Maurice decided it would be a waste not to take advantage of his new found popularity so he duly went about his things enjoying himself to the max but at the same time he kept his relationship with his little monkeys strong.

Now Maurice had been about a year or eighteen months on the market and he wasn't particularly searching for anything and as we all know this is exactly when things actually happen especially when you are not looking for it.

One fine summer's evening Maurice went out with some colleagues to celebrate. As he was contemplating about hitting the hay he began an unexpected chat with a young pretty owl and believe me she was in good shape but on top of that she seemed to quite the clever little owl.

She convinced him to join her and her friends to party into the smaller hours of the night which he accepted. As they walked to the next watering hole he overheard the young owl say in her native tongue *"I have a soft spot for shaved headed monkeys"* now Maurice had been around this language for some time and due to the fact he was an audio learner over the years he had picked up a little bit of the lingo and being the cheeky monkey he is he made his move and this ladies and gentlemen is how Maurice began the next chapter of his life that would lead him in a very different direction.

This was a difficult period for Maurice as he was still having issues with the Mantis but the owl took all of his baggage on board with her and accepted that he had a history. By the way when I say she was young to be honest she was ten years his junior but this didn't seem to deter either of them. She helped him out when he needed physical and mental support but she also backed him in his never ending battle with the Mantis. A year quickly passed by and they moved in together and things seemed to be go like clockwork.

Time passed and Maurice was feeling relaxed and one might say even happy after all he had gone through with the Mantis, Maurice felt he had deserved to be happy too. As things continued an invitation arrived from Maurice's homeland from his older brother inviting him to his wedding but it wasn't going to be easy the wedding was planned to take place in the 'land down under' (Australia).

So they began saving and it wasn't a rudimentary task especially since the owl was a student and had no stable income other than her parents hand me downs but this didn't put them off because Maurice had a plan.

Now I don't know how your memory is but as mine serves me it was the year 2012 and as it had miraculously panned out the European championships were taking place in Poland and the Irish team were handed their group games in two polish cities. Maurice began his clever little idea. He began to contact friends and families back home, at the same time he started contacting flat owners in the two cities where Ireland were due to play their matches and hey

Presto his master plan was beginning to bear fruits.

His idea was to rent Polish flats in the two host cities at a low cost price and maximise his earnings by renting the same flats out to Irish fans that were making their way to Poland for the championships. It worked and soon Maurice was receiving phone calls and emails from Irish fans in need of somewhere to lay their heads after matches and heavy intake of Polish beer and vodka.

He worked day and night tirelessly pushing his limits organising the logistics of it all. It didn't take long before the media back home for wind if his little idea and they began contacting him unceasing his business idea four fold. He was on TV, radio and newspapers. His plan had worked and by the end of the Euros he had successfully with his small troop of workers accommodated over four hundred fans of the green army (COYBIG).

He returned from his endeavours in these polish cities with more than enough to cover the cost for the monkey and his owl girlfriend to go on a trip of a lifetime. They booked their flights with a little detour thorough the land that brought us Gangam Style and kimchi (S.Korea) and eventually onto their final destination of Sydney, Australia a full month before the wedding was scheduled. #result. They toured around, found accommodation, landed short term work and life was good.

Soon after the rest of the entourage had arrived for the impending wedding nuptials on the exotic island of Hamilton which sat due south of the famous Great Barrier Reef.

Koala holding, kangaroo feeding, gun shooting, golf cart driving and Australian celebrity meetings plus the odd bit if sunbathing and swimming and of course the wedding ceremony all took place on their magical time on the island but all good things come to an end. The older brother of Maurice tied the knot to his long term partner in the idyllic surrounding of this stunning little piece of paradise. To say the least all in all it was a fantastic part of the holiday. Soon after they all went their own merry ways.

After a week of being pampered they took to the seas by ferry to the mainland where they stayed a couple of extra nights on the north east coast of Australia before they rented a vehicle and began their journey south on their two thousand and eleven kilometre drive back to Sydney of course stopping off in literally every cool place as possible. The journey back was to say the least pretty interesting, sightseeing many famous Australian towns, cities and beaches and added in for good measure was the occasional argument over such things as to where to eat, money, where to sleep, money, driving rules and money again.

So I'd like to address the title of this chapter because so far it all seems like your regular relationship. As we know owls are known for their wisdom, however when you have a person who believes they know everything even if they haven't experienced the situation in hand then how can you call somebody wise.

See this young lady no matter what the subject no matter what situation would contest everything, now you may say that's just the demeanour of a law student or lawyer which she was, a law student. But when you take into consideration when a young lady of a tender age of nineteen is telling you she knows more about finances, raising kids and dealing with exes even though she never held a serious job or have kids or had never been in a serious relationship then you begin to doubt the wisdom of the so such called wise owl.

See, Maurice had already been in a relationship with a young lady who always felt she was correct and her needs preceded his but in fact this was the last thing he needed in his life. Having a youthful girlfriend was one thing and having a rocking body with a bubble butt and tits to die for was another thing but if the chemistry isn't there and the communication isn't correct then it will never work. Just ask any woman who has been with a good looking man with a six pack if that alone will make the relationship a success. (Just saying)

Now back to the story ☺

After over three months of travelling the couple were back on the plane, becoming members of the mile high club and heading back to Europe and back to reality (oops there goes gravity). (SORRY).

It wasn't long after they had returned to their regular lives that the first ripples of discontent became apparent. Things slowly deteriorated and it began when the young owl told Maurice one evening that she didn't see her future with him because of the same baggage she presumably accepted. Also on top of all those niggling problems they had the wannabe wise owl broke one of the most sacred rules of life and that's never argue with the parents of your partner because its an irreparable bridge but of course the all knowing Owl done exactly that and that was a stone too far for him and his family.

This made Maurice think and he also came to the conclusion that there was no point in avoiding the inevitable and with one swift chop of the axe the relationship was concluded just like this chapter. But he had left this part of his life with more than one life lesson.

1.   Age, which divides us all and creates stereotypes is really just a number and chemistry between people is far more important, however if you are with somebody due to aesthetics then you should re-evaluate why you are with that person.

2.	Acceptance is a rare commodity and if somebody doesn't accept that you have a past then fuck them and they will only end up poisoning you and holding you back.

3.	Always be yourself, not everybody you meet along your path is going to be your friend and if you find that some people are using you as a stepping stone to greater or improve themselves then make a clean break and don't look back.

CHAPTER 7

THE NOT SO INDEPENDENT CAT

Cats (Felis Catus) – spend a large amount of time licking their coats to keep them clean. Cats can be inquisitive, friendly, playful, active, loving and independent. Just remember who is boss; Cats appreciate attention but only when they want it. Most house Cats crave your love and attention, but they prefer they get it on their terms instead of yours Cats are extremely dependent on others and domestiCated Cats rarely survive on their own in the wild.

It is well known Cats will eat their owner if they die and the Cat has no food, just goes to show how they only think about themselves.

Three years with the owl and it was over just like that and there was no looking back for Maurice he had made his decision and it was final. The owl was pretty persistent for sometime but Maurice was adamant in his decision and that was that.

He was back to being a single monkey and he was a free man again and of course he wasn't actively searching for the owls replacement because inside he knew his worth and that life would work its magic so he was calm and relaxed.

On an unextraordinary Thursday evening just as Easter was beginning Maurice and his buddies got together for their for their weekly poker game (which he won as usual) it wasn't a regular game as Maurice for the month leading up to this evening he had decided to go off all alcohol in a bid to see if he was dependant on it or whether he had it under control and to his ease he was now one month dry.

His friends complained that a sober Maurice wasn't as much fun as an intoxicated Maurice and he folded under the peer pressure on the agreement that if he drank that the guys would accompany him to the city centre in search of more fun, which they did ;) After he had inevitably won the game, they set out for the city centre. The first pub they arrived at was as dead as a door nail. The group lost interest quickly but Maurice having started drinking again rallied the troops and promised that the next bar they go to would be a winner and he wasn't wrong. They ended up in one of his favourite watering holes 'The Embassy'

Upon arrival they luckily found a vacant table. Maurice handed out instructions to the crew. ONE guy to the bar, ONE guy to protect the table and the last guy to use the bathroom as needed. Maurice went to the bar, the Scottish terrier guarded the table and the Norwegian yeti hit the jacks. Before I continue I'll give you a quick insight to the Terrier and the Yeti. The Terrier was a gentle and pleasant young Scottish chap who had relocated to Poland because of his partner and worked as a language teacher but to be completely fair he was a bit dim witted no offence to the poor lad it's just he didn't grasp things very quickly.

The Yeti on the other hand was a giant of a man who hailed from Norway and stood at a staggering 6,10ft or in meters 2m10cm and worked as a volleyball coach for the local women's professional team, some would say a gentle giant. All in all they were god lads. It was a practice Maurice took on later in life he would try to surround himself with smart, educated and good people because he had learnt that these are the type of friends that would help you when you needed it the most.

As Maurice reached the bar he turned to see how his instructions were working out. Of course like many times before the terrier had idiotically not listened to a word he had said and was standing behind him with a large foolish grin. As the yeti emerged from the toilet three Cats had sneakily occupied the table that was meant to be the guy's table.

"Ja pierd#@" (Polish swear word) thought Maurice, and he tried to figure out what to do next. He walked towards the table and observed who had taken his table. Three young Cats sat chatting away, what to do next he thought to himself, he noticed that the table was quite large and that it would be possible for all of them to sit there so Maurice tried to build up the confidence to ask if he and his friends could join their table but at the last second chickened out and returned to his mates. The Terrier questioned his motives and called him a pussy for not going through with speaking to the Cat group.

Now if you knew the Terrier the audacity was beyond insulting which spurred Maurice on to try again and this time he wouldn't fail. He dove in head first and asked straight up if he and his friends could join them. To his amazement the pretty Cat on the inside invited him to join them on the agreement that he sat next to her. And this is how Maurice unwillingly met the Cat who would send his life spiralling down another unforeseen rabbit hole.

The night went from surprise to surprise, the Cat really took a liking to Maurice and was sitting close to him asking him lots of questions and she seemed genuinely interested. Now if you remember earlier in the book when Maurice pretended not to understand any Polish? Well he played the same trick again as he listened to what the Cats were saying to each other as he sat there with his two friends.

He heard them saying things like: *"oh he's quite cute"* or *"he seems smart"* and *"will you take his number?"*. Once again he bided his time and then he asked everybody if they wanted to go dancing that he knew a really good club and not too far away. The Yeti at this point decided to make a break for it so now it was only the Terrier and Maurice on the way to the club to try and charm the young Cats with their ancient dance moves :-p

In the club the pretty Cat invited Maurice to dance whilst the Terrier chanced his luck with the other two. On the dance floor Maurice made an advance which the Cat merely ignored but she then told him not so fast....

As the night came to an end they all decided to grab a kebab, Maurice being the gentleman paid for everybody's which entail the Cat decided she would feed him which lead to Maurice getting kebab sauce all over his face but it was playful and she was flirting with him. Ten minutes later the taxi showed up, she gave him her number and told him to contact her after the Easter festivities.

And this ladies and gentlemen is the next part in the history of how Maurice became Maurice.....

They began dating but again it wasn't an easy one. The Cat studied in a different city 2 hours from where Maurice was living. They wanted to be with each other so they began the arduous and long distance relationship. It wasn't easy at first but it got better. The fact the Cat was a medical student meant she had long evenings studying and plenty of lessons and courses but Maurice wanted to make it work so he remained patient.

According to Maurice and he took into consideration all the previous relationships he had been it this one was different this one was special and this one was going to work but there was a specific reason for this and by the end of this chapter it will become evident as to why he believed this.

Maurice had never been happier he had a beautiful, athletic, intelligent new partner who at the same time came from a privileged back round which let's say made life a little bit easier. It allowed them to indulge in the nice things in life which up to this point had never really been an option for Maurice his life in Poland so far had been take it as you can get it (refer to the chapter called 'The Mantis').

They went to the opera, drank good whiskey, ate sushi and Indian and prawns and Maurice thought to himself that finally things had come full circle and that now it was his turn to enjoy life. They travelled to to places like Rome and Budapest and even further abroad to places like Qatar, Singapore, Malaysia and Indonesia. Things were better than it had even been and

Maurice funnily felt they've had met the right partner after so many difficult years trying to do what he thought was best for his little monkeys.

But as Maurice became more serious with the Cat he began to see some cracks in her armour she was holding back in him and not telling him a lot of private information about herself. He seen that in some situations she had reacted quite strangely and not as you would expect. There were simple situations like sitting on a tram or in a taxi and she would begin to panic and lose control and inexplicably needed lingo to the bathroom. Maurice soon found out that she was also having therapy with a licensed psychologist and that she was also taking heavy medication to deal with her mental issues.

The little Cat had some underlying problems and Maurice was soon to find out that these problems all stemmed from her family especially her mum and dad. She believed to the bottom of her heart that her parents were the ideal couple and all she ever wanted in life was to replicate their relationship because to her it was perfect but as we all know ladies in gentlemen there is no such thing as perfection in this twisted existence we call life.

Ok so some details on the perfect couple is only fair wouldn't you agree? And you can be the judge. But don't forget we are all imperfect so before you make your mind up remember the quote from the Bible "cast the first stone he who hasn't sinned". A good lesson in life is to always take things with a pinch of salt ☺. So back to the parents, her father was a hard working man worked every day in his garage fixing cars but because it was a special type of garage and he carries out specific work he was very well paid and had some nice contracts tied up. He worked day in and day out and racked up a lit if tax free cash and during his days off and weekends he played in his band and went to church like clockwork.

He never missed his ban practice and he never missed his Sunday mass which to Maurice was a bit over the top. So that's the daddy now onto the mammy.

Her mother was a well dressed, well spoken and fashionable lady with an eye for extravagant items. She ran her own little private business selling insurance and an estate agency. She also liked to have herself a drink in the evenings especially when her hubby went to his band practice or his beloved church and here ladies and gentlemen you can begin to see the small cracks in this perfect relationship. I'll go into one or two in detail and that will suffice to see that the perfect relationship that the little Cat wanted to build her future foundations on were not so stable.

One evening Maurice and his beautiful Cat returned back to her parents house. Upon arriving the Cats elder sister had just arrived from Norway of all places. She was sitting at the kitchen table with the mother whose eyes were all puffy and red. Maurice knew instantly that this was not a place for him So the Cat joined the mother and sister and Maurice took up refuge in the bedroom waiting for the situation to pass by.

Hours went by and Maurice could hear sobbing coming from the kitchen area and not just of the mother but from all three occupants. He tried to analyse and speculate about what could be going on but when he soon found out it wasn't exactly what he had envisaged.

The Cat returned to the room sobbing gently and embraced Maurice with strength and she wouldn't let go as she cried onto his shoulder taking solace in her partner. Then she sat in silence with a look of despair and disbelief upon her pretty face. Maurice told her to take her time and only tell him if she wanted to and if she was capable of doing so. Then she began talking and what came next shattered the dream of the Cat and what she always believed to be unbreakable and perfect.

The mother had described how violent and how deceitful the father was and how he had been cheating on her for years and that he had had an on/off mistress (from the band) for many a moon. On top of that the mother had told her daughter's tat on one evening whilst visiting friends for a party that she had inadvertently made a joke about the fathers infidelities which nobody took notice of except for the man in question. His reaction was to remain quiet but later he would seek his revenge and seek it he did.

When everybody had gone to bed the father stood up and rose out of bed pulling the mother by her hair to the floor yelling and screaming at this point he began kicking her in the stomach and it's good to point out that two weeks previous to this horrendous night the mother had undergone surgery to remove her womb (hysterectomy). If it hadn't been for the Cat's cousin going to the bathroom and asking if everything was ok after he heard some groaning then the mother believed she may well have just been killed that terrible evening.

The Cat's perception of the perfect family bubble had just been burst and she came crashing back to earth in a very abrupt manner. From that point on she maintained she could never look at her father in the same admiring way that she always had. Her respect for him had evaporated over night. Maurice to the best of his abilities tried to console her but he knew that the only place she could come to terms with this new info was in her safe place with her therapist.

The relationship continued but under a dark cloud whenever they were around her father. She became distant and kept her contact to a bare minimum. It was around this point the father took a disliking to Maurice and began to give him a bit of a cold shoulder. Maurice believed that the father felt that Maurice was taking his place as the patriarchal male and the Cat felt safer with Maurice than her own dad.

On a cold wet April evening the mother and father decided to have a few glasses of whiskey which Maurice had kindly brought them from Ireland. Now up to this point Maurice had never any problems telling people about his little monkeys but the Cat had pleaded with him not to tell her father because she knew he wouldn't approve of his daughter dating a monkey with baggage.

So trying to make her happy he promised not to bring it up in conversations but if he were asked he wouldn't deny his kids existence. The Cat told her friends and her sister and eventually her mother but kept her father in the dark and on this lovely evening the mother let the Cat out of the bag and the father flipped and we all know what that can be like....

Next all Maurice knew was he wasn't allowed to visit their house and he had some issues with the Cat. At first she stood by him and said she was staying with him. Then of course the father made false accusations about the little monkey which she didn't believe at first. Then he sent strange and dangerous men to his flat in the middle of the night pretending to be police officers, they rang his flat number but it was after 10pm and Maurice wasn't expecting any visitors so he choose to ignore it.

Then can a knock on his door which was super strange to him So he quietly looked through the peep hole only to see two men dressed in dark clothing whispering to one another outside with no lights in the hallway. He was genuinely terrified and scared for his life.

The next day Maurice went to the police station to find out what was happening but there was no report at all it was all scare tactics and made up bullshit to scare him away from the Cat and the police officer told him to be careful and to look after himself. Then the father threatened to take away her car and her credit cards and that's what broke the donkeys back and the relationship was over.

He tried his best to try and explain himself to her but she just wouldn't listen to him. She had made her decision and there was no exceptions. This partner who he initially had believed was the woman he was going to marry had just dropped him, blocked him and made he feel invisible and as if their love never happened and that was that he had no other choice but to accept it, which was a difficult task but what else was he to do. Maurice was devastated and inconsolable. He thought it was all over with nowhere to go. What was next particularly since he thought this relationship was the one.

He went to work and hid his anger and sadness but after he went directly home, he stopped eating, visiting friends and going out and wrote sad songs and cried every evening for two months. The only thing that actually stopped him from killing himself was his two little monkeys who he owes his life to. And that was that the not so independent Cat was gone and Maurice's life had taken another unexpected twist and turn.

The moral of this unit is this:

1.   Some things in our lives can't be controlled and will happen no matter how hard we try to stop it. We must learn to cope on our own without the assistance of others as survival training cause you never know when you will have to go it alone.

2.   We are all very different people in comparison to what people see on the outside.

3.   There are so many reasons to be alive and we just have to look for them because they are right in front of us.

And if you keep reading you will read about the people that changed Maurice's life beyond recognition and kept him alive.

CHAPTER 8

THE SHY FISH

Please refer to my last book:

"The silly monkey and the shy fish"

CHAPTER 9

LITTLE MONKEY #1

So now we get to the part of the book which goes into detail about the most important people who have come into Maurice's life and changed it for the better.

These people Maurice can't say or think of enough words to describe his feelings for them, they helped keep him alive in his darkest hours, they made him smile, they made his cry and they make him proud everyday but above all they thought him how to love.

The first one showed their little face on the 01st of August 2007. This was the day that Maurice entered fatherhood and not would it change his life forever and in a way he never even tried to comprehend until he was given no choice in the matter. This was new territory for Maurice because the closest thing he had ever been to being a father was having a new mobile phone and trying to charge it not to scrape it keep it full with money for phone calls and not dropping I guess you could say it's the same as being a dad haha.

Little Aleksander was meant to be little Aleksandra according to all the doctors who scanned Maurice's former partner's belly on at least four occasions. It wasn't until the evening before the caesarean was due to happen, a nurse came into the room for one last scan to see if the baby was in the correct position before the surgery and made a remark: *"Oh a boy, you must be so happy"* unknown to the nurse at the time both Maurice and his partner were expecting a girl and had been shopping for the arrival of a girl. She rang Maurice in a hysterical manner crying and screaming that it's not a girl it's a boy. Maurice just sat back and thought cool the first player for my football team.

Aleksander was born and Maurice became a dad and he couldn't have been happier. Now time has passed.amd young Aleksander has proven to be a very smart young man with a lot of promise especially academically. Maurice watched and observed as his little monkey grew up and he couldn't be prouder.

It's also very evident that Aleks is a very caring kid with a very big heart. He constantly tries to make everybody happy whether it be with his scores form school or his achievements within sports and other activities. But what he doesn't know is that even when he doesn't win a competition or get a five in his grades Maurice couldn't be happier with him because Maurice knows that little Aleks is doing it to make everybody happy. Sometimes however little Aleks puts too much pressure on his young shoulders which is unnecessary (***read this part again Aleks) :-p***

Sometimes Maurice is a little worried for little Aleks that the pressure from his mother requires him to be more mature for his age so this is the reason why Maurice makes sure that every time he speaks to him or meets with him that it's always a fun and pleasurable time for them both. Later in life young Aleks will grow up to be a strong, intelligent, aware young man and he will see the effort Maurice had made during his childhood years and he may well just see through the manipulative ways of the Mantis.

Most importantly Maurice hopes that the little monkey sees that the love Maurice has for him and his bond with him will always be there and will never weaken. Maurice will always be there for him through the good the bad and the difficult times. Also Maurice would like to point out that young Aleks has picked up some of his mother's manipulative skills but they don't work on Maurice.

CHAPTER 10

LITTLE MONKEY #2

Now the next little monkey there was no pre knowledge about whether it was going to be a boy or a girl because the Mantis didn't want to go through the same disappointment as she had with the first kid so they decided to leave it up faith and on the morning of the 21st of April 2009 Maurice added the second little footballer to his team ☺

Little Kryspin (Pinek) was born and little Aleksander (Aleks) had a little brother to take care of and Maurice had more shitty nappies to change ....

If the characteristics of a monkey ever suited a child then this child was Kryspin to a tee. He was energetic and boisterous and giddy and dynamic and he is still to this day. Maurice would say he is a chip off the old block.

This little monkey is a little bit different than the older one as he excels at sports such as football, cycling and skiing even going as far as representing Poland ski cross at the kids world cup. He is a little bit lazy when it comes to the academic side of things but that Maurice believes will come with time.

Little monkey #2 is the cheeky, witty one who likes to make jokes and try to get away with naughty behaviour which is in a way pretty similar to Maurice but at the same time he is a little charmer and women be falling at his feet in a few years time especially because of his big green eyes and long full lashes...

Kryspin has a little devil inside of him according to Maurice which will in the future stand to his favour or in fact go against him. It will take time for him to learn when and when not he should use his skills but of course mistakes will be made. On the other hand the younger of these two little monkeys has a gift with mathematics which surprised the hell out of Maurice one day when they were going to the swimming pool, as Maurice was just about to pay for tickets to enter little Kryspin shared the information that there was a cheaper option and that we would save some money if we done it his way which Maurice did and did in fact save some money.

This little monkey has exactly the same support and love as his elder brother and he should never forget this either and Maurice will always be there for him too.

These two little monkeys have no idea how important they are to Maurice and he would do anything for them.

Now we move onto the last and final person so far in Maurice's life that has made such a huge impact on his life and the next chapter will be entirely dedicated to her.

Aleks and Kryspin, I love you both more than you can ever imagine.

CHAPTER 10

THE ELEGANT GIRAFFE

Giraffe – with those extra long legs it is not **surprising** that a **Giraffe's** neck is too short to reach the ground!

Giraffes have a dark bluish tongue that is very long – approximately 50cm (20 inches). They may be preyed on by lions, leopards, spotted hyenas and African wild dogs. Giraffes are also surprisingly fast with speeds of up to 35 mph. They have a powerful kick that can kill carnivores such as lions and crocodiles. Not to mention the are one of the world's most beautiful and elegant animals ever to grace the face of Earth, heavenly as if sent from God himself.

So Maurice has his two little monkeys in his life and he couldn't be happier with the tough decision he made to remain in Poland and hold his ground. He had always said to himself that no matter how tough the going got for him he would always be there for them and nothing would ever change that.

There was one thing however that he was missing and that was somebody who would stand by him and be in his corner when the shit hit the fan as it occasionally does, that one person that would scratch his back or think about his general happiness. Up to this point Maurice had always looked after himself whether it be physically, emotionally or financially. If you read back through the last few chapters you will see also that he was very capable of doing so but to have that one person that you can always lean on was the one thing that was always on his mind.

As per usual he wasn't hunting for this one person because Maurice was always a firm believer that these types of encounters happened when you least expected it and he wasn't far off.

On a cold Friday evening in January Maurice had made his way to his atelier to begin his regular stint teaching private students English. The second semester had just begun and as per usual some new faces had joined the course. The addition of these new faces was always a nice way to freshen up the classes.

One of the new faces had arrived at Maurice's classroom and he invited her to enter. She immediately blushed and turned bright red the moment he spoke to her and she didn't dare look him in the face. He asked her name and once again eyes facing the ground her face going scarlet she shyly said in a low but very distinctive German accent "Danuta". This ladies and gentlemen is how Maurice met his current partner and wife to be (hopefully).

She sat down opened her book and her copy book and write everything down that Maurice had written on the white board and any new words Maurice had said that she hadn't heard before and not only this she asked questions about pronunciation and for the meanings of the new words too. Maurice immediately could feel that this young lady was very intelligent and wanted to learn and he could see that it was important for her to do so and not waste her time it her money. This made Maurice look at her in a different light he began observing her and he began asking himself what was it about her that was so attractive.

One thing that popped into his head was that she had a longer than average neck length it was more elongated than that of the other students and that made him think of the Karen long neck women in Thailand and the Kayan women of Myanmar. In both societies the longer the neck the more sought after and attractive the women are to the local men and Maurice had just found out that he also had a bit of a fetish for long necks ☺.

He observed her more and more and he also noticed that she would go bright red upon every interaction with anybody in the group including himself which he found utterly irresistible.

Now to Maurice this once monotonous, tiring Friday evening had become exciting and fresh and he couldn't wait to get into classes and his heart beat faster Every time he seen her come into his lesson. In one particular evening the topic of the lesson was "RELATIONSHPS" and Maurice seen this as his chance to find out more about this timid elegant Giraffe. He questioned the group about the meaning of life and about the point of marriage and about whether or not they were currently in a relationship.

Here was his chance, he asked her and she said she was seeing someone and his heart dropped he was to say the least sad upon hearing this news but he then made a joke saying that if he invites her for a drink she would say yes and she responded as quickly as he had made the joke and her response was not what he was expecting **"YOU'RE NOT MY TYPE"** the group burst out laughing and Maurice's confidence took a huge hit but he hit back by asking her what her type was and she clearly stated that she like men with dark hair and dark eyes the exact opposite of Maurice. His heart sunk a little but if you know Maurice this type of let down was never going to stop him.

He was patient and a few months passed by and it was soon coming to the end if the semester and as per semester the regular progress test was looming. Now like I said Maurice had been observing the pretty little Giraffe and he hasn't mentioned it so far but the more he observed he the more attractive he found her. He loved how she went red Every time he spoke to her, he liked how modestly she dressed, he loved how hard working and intelligent she was and damn did he love her ass......

On top of this he also took note that she was always one of the last students to leave lessons and this he was hoping would happen again after the progress test. He hoped that she would be the last student to finish the test which would give him the opportunity to enquire more about her and even possibly invite her for a drink.

The day of the test arrived and it worked out exactly as Maurice had envisioned. The beautiful long necked Giraffe was the last student remaining and Maurice put his plan into action. He first asked how the test was just to get her speaking and not to let's say scare her and this is how the conversation went:

M: So how was the test?

G: Not too bad.

M: Hmm now I have you alone maybe i should lock the door haha.

G: There's still a window I can jump out of (smiling).

M: Haha your boyfriend will kill me if he finds out I locked the door and you had gone escape through a second floor window.

G: (with a strange look upon her face) What boyfriend?

M: I thought you said you have a boyfriend?

G: Let's say it's complicated.

M: What do you mean?

G: He's coming this week and we are going for a wedding but it's not a great situation.

M : If it's still complicated when he leaves here's my full name on Face book why don't you add me and we can go for a drink?

G: Haha (going very red) won't your girlfriend be angry if she finds out?

M: I don't have a girlfriend we broke up!

G: Ok, maybe we can (shyly smiling and very red).

M: Take a picture of my full name and add me and write to me when he leaves.

G: Ok, so see you maybe.

(The reason he had done this was when he searched for her online there were a few people with the same name and none of them had pictures so this was his only chance).

The Giraffe then left the room smiling and Maurice was hopeful that his plan had worked now all he had to do was wait.

Ten days passed and Maurice was beginning to lose hope a little when his phone vibrated. It was what he been waiting for his plan had worked she had added him and they were in contact. He wrote to her and they set up their first date on that Friday at 18.00 in the city centre. She looked beautiful as usual and Maurice knew she didn't know this and she definitely didn't think he thought this every time he seen her. As soon as she reached him her face lit up bright red, he gave her a kiss on the cheek and they headed for a cafe.

They drank and they talked over coffee then Maurice invited her to another bar close by. They sat down he enquired what tickled her fancy drink wise and she said water, he tried to convince her to have a glass of wine but she politely refused. He had a little plan, he went to the bar ordered a karafka of wine and returned to their table. She asked where her water was and he replied with a cheeky grin: *"I think the waitress misunderstood my bad polish"* ☺

They continued until about 10pm all the time she was speaking in polish and he in English which for a lot of people would be strange but the two of them were very comfy with this. Maurice popped up from the table as he head to the toilet and as he left he gave her a gently kiss on the cheek making her blush and smile.

He walked her to bus soon after and that was the end of their first date. It was a long time coming but in his mind it was totally worth it and he began planning when he would see her again.

The next he got in touch immediately and he asked her about her plans that day. Now it was a wet and grey overcast Saturday and not a day for walking or spending time outside. She responded saying she didn't have any plans so Maurice cordially invited her round to his flat for a glass of wine and a second date. She said she needed to think about it but within an hour she asked Maurice for his address and not long after she was knocking on his door. He was excited he was already on a second date with this stunning Giraffe and he couldn't believe his luck.

They chatted and chatted and drank wine and all the time Maurice was flirting and touching her and occasional trying to give her little kisses. He kissed her cheek and he kissed her forehead but every time he tried to kiss her lips she let him for a microsecond and then she would pull away and go all red. But Maurice was persistent and he kept trying and eventually he got what he sought after he got that first kiss. Now because Maurice is a gentleman and gentlemen never kiss and tell this is as much info as you shall be getting about this particular evening however I can say it was everything he ever expected and more it was special and he knew it, he felt it and he wasn't wrong it was the beginning of something very rare between two people.

As the evening ended Maurice had informed the cure little Giraffe that the next morning he had an early flight so once again he found himself walking her to her bus stop and kissing her goodnight but this was about to be a test because Maurice was enough to leave for work for the next 6-8 weeks. The question was what would come from their two dates together??

The next morning Maurice jumped on a plane and flew to Switzerland to commence his work but one thing he knew he was going to do was stay in touch every single day because he knew it was the smart thing to. She was so beautiful and smart and funny and she wasn't in bad shape either. Every day he video called her and he told her about his days and what he was doing and he asked her about her.

This went on for the entire four weeks of his time in Switzerland. When he was coming close to the end if his time there he received a phone call from a friend I the UK who needed his assistance training his teachers. He rang the Giraffe and he told her about the extra two week job but he told her he would only take the job off she visited him in the UK and she agreed. Now

Maurice was on the move again and this time to the UK but he knew his pretty little Giraffe would come visit him which made him smile. Maurice landed in London and got to work. He kept up the daily contact and within a week he was travelling out to the airport to meet the gorgeous Giraffe.

It was a surreal feeling the woman who uses to be his student who according to her he wasn't her type who he had only been on two dates with had travelled thousands of kilometres across Europe was just about to touch down in the UK. WOW......

This was a massive step forward in the physical part of the relationship, they literally had two dates and then the other two months had been completely on line through video chat and messages. For Maurice this was the beginning of the physical relationship. He gave her the grand walking tour of London, showing her to Buckingham Palace, Hyde Park, Big Ben and Parliament and the London Eye of course. That evening they jumped on a train and made their way to the south coast of England where Maurice had taken up residence.

He had rearranged his room to make the pretty little Giraffe comfortable. They went for walks, the talked and they went shopping during her brief visit to the UK but it was enough for Maurice to begin falling in love with her. He had met somebody who would become very dear to him. Soon after he returned to London and he bid farewell to his new friend as she jumped on a coach to bring her to the airport to Catch her flight back to Poland. Maurice jumped on his train a little bit sad that she had left but a whole lot happier thinking about what was to come.

A quick visit back to Ireland to say hello to the family and then in a plane back to Poland to pick up where he had left off with the stunning Giraffe. Now when he got back he had nowhere to stay so the Giraffe told him they he couldn't say no and that he was to shack up with her before his big move to the big smoke the capital of Poland Warsaw. Just so you know that before Maurice had flown to Switzerland where was head hunted by a large American corporate firm and the position was in Warsaw and when he accepted the job back then he never could have expected the turn of events with the Giraffe so he didn't really have a choice cause he had a contract for one year signed.

The next two months Maurice shacks up with the pretty little Giraffe and the built an unbreakable relationship which went from strength to strength. He looked for her every day and when she came home from work dinner was always prepared and set out on the table not only that he always made extra so she could bring some to work for her lunch. Things went from better to better and Maurice's feelings grew stronger and stronger but then came the day when he had to make the big move and he packed up his few things and moved to Warsaw.

This was to be the greatest test Maurice had ever put himself. Away from his new lover and away from his little monkeys than he had even been. Ten years he had toiled and troubled to be in the kids' lives, ten years he had gone through many hardships to know his kids and for them to know him.

Ten years was a long time and now he had changed locations and he was five hundred kilometres away something he had never tried before and it was going to be tough. Not only that he was away from his new girlfriend the one who had been so patient with him and the one he really wanted to make work this time. He said to her and to his kids that even though he was on the other side of the country it wouldn't stop him from seeing them and this he promised.

He worked every day from 08.00 until 21.00 and on Fridays he would finish a little earlier in order to catch his 21.00 bus across the country every weekend to see her and to see the kids. It took its toll as Maurice had two jobs and he was running around the city everyday and then on top of it all he would take bus five hours stay for two days and then travel back five hours and go directly to work. He enjoyed the experience he gained and he also made some new friends but the hold Wroclaw had a Maurice was never going to make him stay in Warsaw his heart and everything he held dear to him was there too.

The Giraffe stayed with him through this difficult transition and was always supportive of his decisions, she stayed patient awaiting his return which was imminent. Maurice and the

Giraffe started planning their future together once he had decided that he was moving back and they began house hunting.

After a couple of months looking at places they finally choose a place where they would move in together after all this time they had been apart they were making up for lost time.

The next couple of months the two of them were shopping and investing and painting and knocking down walls and shopping and more painting until the shell of a flat was what they could both call home and finally Maurice and the beautiful Giraffe moved in together. Two years together majority of it apart but finally faith and Destiny and hard work and a lot of love and sweat and tears they were officially living together.

After all these years Maurice had finally put all his trust in a woman he felt was going to stand by him no matter what happens, no matter his past or his previous relationships. She was going to be there and share in the good moments but also in the bad and to this point she has done exactly that and he sees no reason as to why that would change and if it does it will only be for the better.

Since they moved in they have gone on to make each other happy and Maurice can't see himself ever being more content. The Giraffe has taught him So many things like humility and humbleness and how to be a better man. She has shown him that happiness doesn't always come from having money or having materialistic items but from the people around you who love you name who care about you and who want only the best for you.

She has also taught him how to be tidier in general 😄. He owes her a debt he can never repay because this ladies and gentleman is the type of man Maurice wants to be moving forward he doesn't want to return to the days of old when he sought attention and he sought out trouble.

Because if this the next unit in the book is dedicated to the person and man and father and friend and partner Maurice wants to be in the future. He now knows that from now on in this journey of life he will meet many a character who may well change many of his thoughts or ideas about certain things but he believes he has finally come of age and it's time to make that a permanent fixture.

The things we can take from this last chapter is that things do really come full circle. If you look at some of the things Maurice had to endure before he finally found out who and what he had to be in order to be happy you could easily say he could have quit a long time ago and feel sorry for himself and to give up.

See in my humble opinion there will be ups and downs and forgive the old cliché but you have to take the good with the bad you have to keep your head high no matter the situation, you will without a doubt encounter obstacles that will nearly defeat you but it's about being brave. If you don't risk you will never know and this is one statement that Maurice lives by and swears by but don't believe me just ask Maurice yourself. Some people will say that they have feelings they can't control or master and that's why we all need a good friend or friends to help us out if these dark places. Maurice has found his friend and he plans in keeping her close so they can go through the darkness together.

CHAPTER 11

THE PROPOSAL

A plan or suggestion, put forward for consideration by others.

1."a set of **proposals for** a major new high-speed rail link"

An offer of marriage.
2. "surely a woman as beautiful as you has had proposals?"

So how does one go about keeping the precious things in life we hold so dearly?

Some put it in the bank, others invest it, some keep it in a safe secret place at home but what if the thing you hold so dear is not a thing or an object but an amazing person, your best friend, your rock when you need help, that person who scratches your head or makes you hot tea with lemon and honey when you are sick and who systematically gives you your medication for an illness and you need not even think about it?

See this is where Maurice is right now, he couldn't be more in love with the pretty Giraffe and he couldn't be happier. The first time in his life he is comfortable, he is content and he feels safe, the first time in his life he feels in control and he makes decisions himself. See most guys can't say these things cause they are scared or embarrassed what their peers might think of them but Maurice doesn't care about that. His little monkeys have a great relationship with the Giraffe too. He sees them asking her questions and planning their time and days with her and of course laughing and making jokes at Maurice's expense but it's all good.

See when Maurice looked at her he sees so many things. On the outside he sees this beautiful, elegant, shy Giraffe but in the inside he sees so much more. He sees her intelligence, her caring side, her loving side, the side of her who wants to take care of him and help him and be close to him. He sees his best friend, his Grazyna to his Janusz (polish joke). Above all he sees the woman he wants to spend the rest of his life with, the woman he wants to travel with, laugh with, grow old with and be happy with. He couldn't imagine his life without her. Things right now couldn't be better so as they say *"why fix it if it ain't broken"*

CHAPTER 12
THE FUTURE

noun: **the future**

A period of time following the moment of speaking or writing; time regarded as still to come.
"We plan on getting married in the near future"

So now we have reached the penultimate chapter. What now for Maurice, I guess only the future will tell, for sure he will have many more ups and downs but at least this time he knows he has somebody who has his back, he knows he has as you say his partner in crime which makes the prospect of the future a positive looking one and he's not afraid to face what comes next.

See this book was written as a way of looking at myself introspectively and I can honestly say it has really had a meaningful effect. I used to be worried and concerned about what others thought about me when in fact I should have been looking at myself and caring about what I thought about myself. Writing this book has given me the confidence and belief in myself and not some made up false impression of who I really am. Having looked back into my past to find out how I got to this point in my life was like a breath of fresh air.

To self analyse myself was something I never imagined doing when I started the first page and to be completely honest to write a second book never mind a first is something I never even considered until it just happened. Don't get me wrong I'm not saying everyone should write a book, what I'm trying to say is that by looking at your decisions made and friends and foes and by taking the positives and the negatives into your stride then I fully believe you too.

you will benefit greatly from doing so and you will come full circle. I was never good at expressing feelings which I believed only made me weak because growing up as a young man to express your emotions was a sign of frailty as a sign of weakness and so I avoided doing so.

In this book I have addressed all the things that made me who I am whether they be positive or negative. Some people may still not accept me but that's their problem and they have to live with that not me and as a consequence they are the ones who will feel negative and uneasy around me whilst I shall not.

I am the master of my own destiny and therefore I will succeed and if u fail I will not lay down and accept it I will stand up again and try again as Maurice has done so many a time over the years. I earnestly encourage you to do the same as it will be a testament to yourself.

Lastly accepting your past and yourself is vital to understanding who you are and who you want to be. People say we should keep toxic people at arm's length but these same people help create who we are help build our morals and they also show us firsthand what we can be and what we can strive to be. What we so in life us up to us not others, we will make good and bad decisions along the way but whatever the outcome we have to accept and take whether it be good or bad.

I hope that reading my trials and tribulations that maybe you can take something from this with you and if not then this is your prerogative. But just sit there and retrace and remember, pause for a moment, think about some of the positives and the negatives which have touched your life, think about the people you have encountered, positive albeit negative, about the people who you once loved or hated about the people who have give you good and bad advice about the exams you passed or failed about the competitions you won or lost about the people who have passed away and become only a distant memory and be thankful because without all of these things, situations and people you would not be the person that is reading this book today.

Nobody really knows why we are here and for what purpose but at least we can understand who we are and why. I guess that's the least we can do for ourselves cause knowing who you are and how you got there will give you some insight as to who you are going to be and this will be your legacy cause this will be passed on through the next generations to come. And to finish, we all want what's best for the ones closest to us.

Thank you for taking the time to read the short history of Maurice, I'm sure in time to come there will be a second edition of his history as there are many more years to live, many more people to meet, as is there time, plenty of time for more great things to happen and for more mistakes but hopefully nothing like the ones that Maurice has made before in his younger years. See believing mistakes won't happen is to say the least slightly naive it's all about being able to deal with anything life can throw at you and take it all in your stride.

I am sure that majority of these reading this will make their own opinion and may even judge Maurice for his actions but whom here amongst us hasn't made a mistake. Mistakes are part and parcel of life and these mistakes make us who we are today. Whether a mistake has thought us something or whether it has made us scared of something it has in the long run a direct correlation to who you are now reading this book.

Have a look back, have a think if you wish, who knows you may just see or find a reason as to why you are who you are, why you behave the way you behave, why you think the way you think or many other answers to questions you may have about yourself.

I hope you have enjoyed reading.

" A BRIEF HISTORY OF MAURICE"

THE END